Split Travel Guide

Sightseeing, Hotel, Restaurant & Shopping Highlights

Sara Laing

Copyright © 2015, Astute Press
All Rights Reserved.

No part of this publication may be reproduced, stored in a retrieval system, or transmitted, in any form or by any means without the prior written permission of the publisher, nor be otherwise circulated in any form of binding or cover other than that in which it is published and without similar condition being imposed on the subsequent purchaser.

If there are any errors or omissions in copyright acknowledgements the publisher will be pleased to insert the appropriate acknowledgement in any subsequent printing of this publication.

Although we have taken all reasonable care in researching this book we make no warranty about the accuracy or completeness of its content and disclaim all liability arising from its use.

Table of Contents

Split 5
   Culture 8
   Location & Orientation 9
   Climate & When to Visit 12

Sightseeing Highlights 15
   Diocletian Palace & Peristil 15
   Cathedral of Saint Dominìus (St. Duje Cathedral) 16
   Veli Varos (Old Split) & Marjan Hill 17
   Museum of Croatian Archaeological Monuments 18
   Hvar Island 19
   Brač Island 20
   Ivan Meštrović Gallery 21
   Croatian National Theatre 22
   Split Aquarium 23
   Bačvice Beach 24
   Dino Park 24
   Krka National Park 25

Recommendations for the Budget Traveller 27
   Places to Stay 27
      Raspudic 27
      Zara 28
      Stambuk 28
      Loza 29
      Milla 30
   Places to Eat & Drink 30
      Zlatna Vrata 30
      Kod Joze 31
      Nostromo 32
      Buffet Fife 32
      Makro Vega 33
   Places to Shop 34
      Fish Market (Peškarija) 34
      Green Market (Stari Pazar) 35
      Marmontova Shopping Street 35
      Joker 36

City Center One 37

Split

Split is the leading city of the Dalmatian region of Croatia and is the economic centre of the beautiful eastern Adriatic. It features a delightful historical centre with Roman walls, temples and squares. Split once housed a palace for the retired Roman emperor Diocletian. With its narrow streets and hidden treasures, Split is the second largest city in Croatia.

The nickname for Split is the "Mediterranean flower" and the "most beautiful city in the world". With easy road transport to Dubrovnik and good ferry links to nearby islands like Hvar and Brač, the city is accessible to visitors to the emerging tourist destination of Croatia.

Most of the city centre is traffic free with park and ride services available from the outskirts. The historical centre of Split is quite small and accessible by foot so take a stroll to see the city's ancient monuments.

The Diocletian Palace in the Old Town is located at the heart of Split. The heavily fortified military stronghold and palace has impressed visitors for centuries and is one of the most imposing ruins you will encounter.

Within the palace walls are over two hundred homes housing over 3000 residents who string their washing from balcony to balcony as they have done for centuries. Below the flapping sheets, children play street games in the ancient passageways.

Just outside of the palace walls on the western side is the Trg Republike. This vast square is enclosed on three sides by neo-Renaissance buildings known as the Prokurative. In the cooler months the square is peaceful and in the summer this is the pulsing centre of activity. The biggest event held here is the Entertainment Musical Festival of Split and many other cultural events and concerts bring the square to life with colour and noise.

Split's Riva Promenade and waterfront is packed most hours of the day and night and there are many bars and cafés in this area.

The climate is good, the people are friendly and, although retaining the feel of a working town, there is plenty to keep visitors entertained in Split.

For adventure lovers Split offers spearfishing, whitewater rafting, rock climbing, hunting, cycling and horse riding.

There are many national parks nearby and visits to the Krka Wayerfalls, Kornati National Park and Plitvice Lakes are some of the more popular day trips from Split.

The Dalmatian coastal cities of Omis, Trogir and Sibenik are close enough for a day trip. Inland Dalmatia is quite different from the coast and a trip to Trijl and Sinj are only a 30-minute drive away.

There are many opportunities along the Riva waterfront to try the excellent wines of Dalmatia that are starting to hit the world markets. Wine bars are popping up everywhere and with 130 grape varieties in Croatia it is easy to see why. For an alternative to wine visitors should try the locally made soft drinks of Orela and the fizzy orange drink Pipi, which has achieved "cult" status.

Another drink to try is Rakija, sometimes called Croatian firewater depending on the strength and used for many types of social gatherings. Weddings, funerals and parties of all kinds usually see a bottle or two appear. Made from a variety of distilled fruit and herbal spirits, many households have their own recipe will offer you a shot of Rakija.

Local food specialities include a variety of risotto dishes which include white rice flavoured with black calamari or tender scampi. There are many Dalmatian and Istrian hams to sample as well as the salty sheeps milk cheese from the island of Pag.

One of the most famous delicacies is soparnik which originates from the nearby Poljica region. This tasty dough snack is filled with a root vegetable called mangold, brushed with garlic and olive oil and baked on a stone fireplace. Similar to a large pizza in size, soparnik is traditionally cut into diamond shapes. You will see Soparnik stalls everywhere.

The residents of Split love sports and the outdoor life as well as their history and culture. The football team of HNK Hajduk Split has not just ordinary fans but devotees throughout Dalmatia and a number of world-class footballers have come from the country. Try to see a derby match against Dinamo Zagreb at the Poljud stadium to witness the fierce loyalty of the local fans.

Tennis is another favourite sport and former Wimbledon champion Goran Ivanisevic comes from Split.

Culture

Music festivals abound in Split and the year culminates with the biggest dance party in Europe, the Silvestre Salsa on New Year's Eve, brings to a close another 365 days of hectic fun and loud music.

The Split carnival is held in the days leading up to Lent (usually in February). This is a short carnival and in two nights the streets and plazas come alive with fireworks, parades and concerts as locals dress in colourful and often outrageous costumes for this long-standing tradition.

Every May hip-hop music and extreme sports bring a certain vibe to the city with DJ sessions, graffiti art, BMX, breakdancing and funky music events.

During the early summer the cult cinemas of Zlatna Vrata and Kino Bačvice in the palace walls and on the beach respectively show alternative films. This is accompanied by a carnival atmosphere as well as exhibitions and parties.

The Split Summer Festival runs from mid-July to mid-August and has recently celebrated its half-century anniversary. Across the city the pretty squares and historic venues come alive for all to enjoy a memorable night under the Croatian skies.

The Ultra Europe electronic music festival in July attracts 60,000 dance fans for three unforgettable days of boat parties, fancy dress parties, poolside madness and dancing in the Poljud Stadium. The event ends with a mammoth beach party.

If you prefer dressing up and period type pageants then try to visit in August. The inhabitants of Split dress in togas and for ten days festivals take place around the Diocletian palace. Emperor Diocletian manages to put in an appearance every year. Dressed in full period costume he addresses his minions in the Peristil Square before being carried to to his bedchamber.

Location & Orientation

Split lies on the shores of the Adriatic Sea and is the second largest city in Croatia. The city has the Roman Palace of the Emperor Diocletian as its focal point and spreads out over a central peninsula. At sea level there are links to the Apennine peninsula and many beautiful Adriatic islands while in the western part of the peninsula the Marjan Hill rises to 178m with far-reaching views.

In the city of Split there are eight settlements that are home to 178,000 people. 96% of these are Croats and 86% of the population is Roman Catholic.

Three very distinctive and separate groups of people inhabit Split. The Fetivi are the actual natives of the city, who take pride in its history and keeping alive their traditional speech, which was derived from the Chakavian dialect.

The second group are the 20th century immigrants who arrived from the nearby Adriatic islands known as the Boduli. The third group is the Shtokavian-speaking immigrants from the Zagora hinterland. This group is known as the Vlaji and their arrival after World War II changed the ethnic characteristics of the city given their numbers.

Once upon a time the city was buzzing with factories and work was plentiful. Industries included plastics, textiles, chemicals, food and paper with the biggest employment being in shipbuilding. This was during the Yugoslavian era. The global recession caused problems in Split and the city is recovering its economic ground.

The Brodosplit shipyard is the biggest local employer with 2,300 workers and it is the largest shipbuilder in Croatia. 350 vessels have been built in the shipyard with 80% being exported.

Getting to Split whether is fairly easy. 20km away from the city, Split Airport in Kaštela receives over a million and a half passengers every year. There are excellent connections to European cities including Munich, Rome and Zagreb. In the winter season many flights from the UK will involve one stopover while in the summer direct flights are available.

There are dedicated airport buses that run to the city centre every 30 minutes from either the terminal or a short walk across the car park will bring you to the local bus stop. There is no train connection from the city to the airport although plans are being made to extend the suburban line.

The Port of Split has daily coastal routes to Ancona in Italy as well as Dubrovnik and Rijeka and in the summer months to Pescara. Many of the Dalmatian islands like Hvar are only accessible by ferry from Split. The port is the third busiest in the Mediterranean and is used by four million passengers annually and some 260 cruise ships call in every year.

Travelling by road is an efficient way to get around Split. The A1 motorway passes through the city as does the Adriatic Highway making access to and from other towns fast and trouble free.

Buses are one of the most popular means of transport for locals and the local bus company Promet Split uses a fleet of Mercedes Benz and MAN vehicles. In most cases you pay on the bus in local currency or Euros. Some bus drivers will only accept the correct amount so bring small coins.

Long distance buses start at 06.00 daily for destinations such as Sarajevo, Trieste, Belgrade and other major cities in Austria and Germany.

Split is the southernmost point on the Croatian Railway network and the journey to Zagreb or Rijeka takes about 5 hours from Central Station. The Split Suburban Railway has one line running between the city harbour and Kaštel Stari.

Bike rental is a good way of getting around the city. Several companies rent out bikes. A day tour by bike and ferry to some of the neighbouring islands is a good way of exploring the area with ferries leaving every couple of hours for Vis, Hvar, Solta and Brac.

Climate & When to Visit

Split sees more than 2,600 hours of sunshine every year.

In the spring the temperatures rise from 8°C in March to a high of 22°C in June. This is a great time to visit as the weather is pleasant and the throngs of summer visitors have yet to arrive.

Summer is pleasantly hot with little rain. With a low of 19°C and a high of 30°C summer this is a great time to take advantage of the beautiful beaches and watersports. In July and August the sea temperature averages around 25°C so is just right for a cooling dip to escape the heat.

As the summer heat fades away, September can be another lovely time to visit as the leaves begin to fall and the daytime temperature averages 25°C. November is the wettest month in Split when it rains on average for 12 days. It is still relatively warm at the end of November with a high of 9°C.

In the winter, the north wind and the wind chill factor can sometimes make Split feel extremely nippy. The *Bura* wind can reduce an air temperature of 5°C to -10°C, so be prepared if visiting in winter. If the wind isn't blowing, Split has a high of 11°C and a low of 5°C in the winter season.

Snow is rare in Split with maybe one day in January and two in February seeing a light covering. Unusually heavy snowfall in February 2012 did cause major traffic problems but on average this only happens every 30 years.

SPLIT TRAVEL GUIDE

Sightseeing Highlights

Diocletian Palace & Peristil

Split
Tel: +385 21 483 674

The historic centre of Split has been built round the remains of the palace and it is easy to see why the palace is on the UNESCO World Heritage List. There are many different parts to explore including the central open air Peristil, the mausoleum with its 24 columns and the 13th century choir with its beautiful Romanesque seating.

The main streets of cardo and decumanus are very well preserved can be wandered around at leisure along with most of the rest of the palace. The Romans used a grid system when creating their roads and the decumanus was the main street from east to west with the cardo being the main north to south road.

Of particular interest are the four monumental gates; Golden, Silver, Iron and Bronze. The Silver Gate on the eastern side of the palace gives access to the Peristil, which is the open-air central area of the palace. The palace might be from Roman times but the many Gothic and Renaissance buildings that have been added over the centuries enrich the feeling of grandeur.

One of the best ways to access the palace is via the basement halls on the sea-side. As you mount the massive steps into the heart of the palace you can't fail to be impressed by the cathedral and the various Roman monuments. The cavernous cellars were originally used as dumps through the Middle Ages but are now filled with stalls offering souvenirs and handicrafts.

Visitors pay a nominal fee if they wish to enter the basement of the palace to see the excavation works.

Cathedral of Saint Dominìus (St. Duje Cathedral)

Kraj Sv. Duje 5
Split
Tel: +385 21 342 589

The cathedral is located inside the palace walls and it is primarily used as a place of worship with mass held daily. The traditional procession of St. Dujam is held on May 7th each year and attracts over one and a half million spectators.

Visit the bell tower for astounding views across the city of Split and over the Marjan Hills. A climb up the 200 metal stairs is worth it. The best time to go is just before sunset.

The white limestone and marble bell tower is a landmark in Split and very easy to find and makes a good reference or meeting point. It is housed in the mausoleum of the Diocletian Palace and is one of the oldest cathedrals in Europe. The entrance fee to climb the bell tower is 15kn.

Veli Varos (Old Split) & Marjan Hill

Veli Varos is the area of Split where many of the fishermen and peasants lived in the 17th century. Many of the traditional peasant houses can still be see today in the maze of pedestrian streets which wind round the many churches and up Marjan Hill.

Look for houses with old stables and wine cellars on the ground floor and an external staircase leading up to the accommodation above. Many of the streets are so narrow that if you stand in the middle you can touch both sides with outstretched arms.

To the west of the city, Marjan is seen as an oasis for the inhabitants who want to walk, cycle, jog and escape the city. The peak is Telegrin and stands at 174m giving wonderful views of the city and across to the mountains of Kozjak and Mosor. Marjan Hill is completely surrounded by the city of Split and the sea and the slopes are covered with a green carpet of Mediterranean pines.

There are many jogging trails and marked walks on Marjan Hill and it has become a romantic retreat and picnic spot. Marjan is the green lung of Split and construction is forbidden on the hills.

Records show that the first mention of Marjan Hill was in the 8th century when it was known as Marulianus. The south side of Marjan is home to the Madonna of Bethlehem church and the beautiful St. Jeronimus church.

Museum of Croatian Archaeological Monuments

Stjepana Gunjace bb, Split
Tel: +385 21/ 323-901
www.mhas-split.hr/

The museum dates from 1890 but didn't actually open in Split until 1976 when the collections were finally displayed in a purpose built complex.

It is a pleasant 20 minute walk to the museum to the north of the old town and there is plenty to see including monuments and artefacts from the old Roman colonies of Narona and Salona.

There are around 3000 stone sculptures and assorted pieces most of which are from the Early Middle Ages. A lot of these relics have come from churches and are extremely intricate with bas-relief motifs and compositions with iconographic content.

Numismatists will be keen to see the superb coins in the museum including examples from the Modern World as well as the antique collections. The Byzantine collection is the most valuable and includes 47 gold coins.

More valuable items can be seen in the 5000 piece jewellery collection; of special interest are the gold and silver earrings found in the Holy Saviour's graveyard in Cetina and also in Koljani.

There are collections of jewellery, weapons and stone artefacts from old Croatian churches as well as many daily use items and a large collection of Croatian Latin epigraphic monuments.

The opening hours are Monday to Friday 9am until 1pm and 5pm until 8pm. Saturday 9am until 2pm and closed on Sundays and public holidays.

There are plenty of places to park near the museum but the local buses stop close by. Photos can be only taken if you ask permission from the director of the museum. The museum is disabled friendly.

Hvar Island

In the height of the summer season (July and August), boats depart five times a day from Split to Hvar and three times a day the rest of the year. A single ticket is around 42kn to the town of Stari Grad on the north of the island. The town of Hvar is small and pretty with expensive yachts moored in the harbour. For many years Hvar was home to the Venetian Empire navy.

Hvar is about 70km in length with an area of 297 sq km. and has fresh water springs and a very fertile coastal plain. The karst landscape and hillsides are covered in vineyards, pine forests, fruit orchards, olive groves and lavender fields.

Once upon a time the most popular exports from the island were wines and rosemary and lavender for the French perfume industry. In the 20th century a major phylloxera blight affected the European wine industry and many islanders left to seek work elsewhere.

Tourism now plays a large part in the newfound prosperity of Hvar and the island is often recommended by Conde Nast.

St. Stephen's Square is the focal point on the island and is open to the sea. This is one of Europe's leading outdoor party venues and young visitors flock here in the summer months.

Look out for the poster made by the schoolchildren of Hvar declaring "everybody is welcome in our town".

Brač Island

There are ten daily crossings from Split to Brač and the journey takes about an hour from Split to the town of Supetar. The last ferry back to Split leaves at 10.45pm and a return ticket costs around 70kn with no time restrictions. Bicycle or scooter rental is quite easy on the island and is a good way of getting around.

The island is the largest of the central Dalmatian islands and covers just under 400 sq km. Much of the island consists of dolomite and limestone and for many centuries the quarries have supplied the materials for decorative stonework.

Many amphitheatres, palaces and temples all across Dalmatia are built from Brač stone. The quarries are found around Postira, Splitska, Pucisca, Donji Humac and Selca and stone was taken from the island to build the White House in Washington, D.C. in the United States.

The island has crystal clear seas and beautiful beaches as well as a rich historical heritage. Livestock breeding and fishing are two of the major activities on the island and this means the restaurants are kept well stocked with the freshest of produce. Local wines, olive oil, almonds and sour cherries are some of the other products from the island.

Ivan Meštrović Gallery

Setaliste Ivana Mestrovica 46
21000 Split
Tel: +385 21 340 800
www.mdc.hr/

Ivan Meštrović's intention was to build a summer home when he bought a piece of land west of Split in the 1920s. His plans for the villa grew however into a working studio and exhibition space as well as his family home. The villa was designed by the sculptor himself and he was involved in the construction. The family lived here until 1941 until Zagreb called and Meštrović left Split.

The generous donation of his villa and much of his works in 1952 to the Republic of Croatia meant that the Ivan Meštrović Gallery was founded and his works were put on show for the public to enjoy. The original collection grew from 70 pieces over the years with purchases and family donations until the Croatian War of Independence and the poor condition of the villa meant it had to close.

Renovations and refurbishments resulted in the new gallery opening in 1998 with nearly all of the work that Ivan Meštrović created now located under one roof. Nearly 600 drawings, 292 architectural plans, 192 sculptures, 4 paintings and a couple of sets of furniture are now on public display. There are also 168 works of art owned by the heirs of Ivan Meštrović.

From the 1st May until 30th September the gallery is open Tuesday to Sunday from 9am to 7pm. From the 1st October until 30th April the hours are Tuesday to Saturday 9am to 4pm, Sunday 10am to 3pm. Closed Monday and public holidays all year round.

The entrance fee is 30kn for adults and 15kn for children. Organised tours can be booked in advance and an audio guide in English is available if you would prefer to wander at your own pace. Permission to take photographs must be requested. There is a small museum shop selling a variety of reproductions and souvenirs.

Croatian National Theatre

1 Gaje Bulata Square, Split
Tel: +385 21 34 49 99
www.hnk-split.hr/

The symmetrical creamy yellow painted building that houses the Croatian National Theatre meant it was the biggest theatre in southeastern Europe when it was completed in 1893.

At the time the theatre had a capacity of 1000 when the population of the town was only 16000. Even now it is one of the oldest and biggest theatres in Croatia.

In 1970 the building was damaged in a fire and the rebuilding lasted some ten years until the grand reopening in May 1980.

There are 300 performances every year with around 40 ballets, opera and dramatic productions as well as symphony concerts by the theatre's orchestra.

Split Aquarium

Obala pomoraca, 21211 Vranjic, Split
Tel: +385 21 247 115
www.aquariumsplit.com/

Split Aquarium is easy to find at Vranjic a few kilometres outside the centre of the city. This is the largest marine aquarium in Croatia and everyone can share in the exciting world under the Adriatic Sea.

The aquarium has 22 tanks with 130 different species on view and these include sharks, moray eels, stingrays, and lobsters. There is also the chance to see freshwater fish, crocodiles and turtles.

The opening times are 10am until 7pm daily, including weekends. The admission prices are 75kn for adults and 50kn for children aged between 4 and 14 years.

Bačvice Beach

To find this beach follow the waterfront in a southerly direction from the bus station. Bačvice Beach is where the locals go and there are many cafés and inexpensive ice cream parlours.

Look out for the popular beach game of Picigin which originated in Split in 1908. This is played with a small ball and in the summer a world championship tournament is held in Split. The game is played in the shallow water and the idea is to keep the small ball from hitting the water. A team of five is usual and there is much diving and running in an attempt to keep the tennis ball in the air.

Dino Park

Vukovarska bb, Omis 21310, Croatia
Tel: + 385 99 444 1234
www.dinopark-croatia.com/

Lovers of all things prehistoric should take the 17km drive from Split to Omis to the Dino Park with its life size moving dinosaur figures; some up to 7m high and 21m in length.

It is an easy drive along the coast road and with the ocean so close it is easy to combine a trip with few hours at the beach.

Other attractions include a pirate ship, a tourist train, trampolines, a merry-go-round and bungee jumping. Kids can have a go at fossil excavation or watch a film in the dino-cinema.

There is free Wifi throughout the park and the fast food restaurants and cafés have dinosaur-themed menus.

Peak season is from the 1st of July until 31st August from 9.30am until 2pm and then from 5.30pm until 10pm. The admission fee is 100kn for children and 60kn for adults.

Low season is the 23rd of May until the 30th of June and the 1st of September until the 14th of September. Prices in low season are 60km for children and 40 for adults. In low season Dino Park is open from 10am until 5pm but does stay open longer weather permitting.

Krka National Park

Lozovac, Croatia
Tel: +385 22 201 777
www.npkrka.hr/

The beautiful national park of Krka is about an hour and half driving time from Split and it is worth making the trip by public transport or on a guided tour.

Some guided tours stop at the small towns of Sibenik by the sea and the superb vantage point at Trogir for some memorable photos.

The small park is a pleasant way to spend a day and the Roški slap or "vast waterfall" is the main attraction. The waterfall crashes down some 15m into the Visovac Lake where there is a designated swimming area which is popular in the summer months.

The park has an excellent information centre at Skradin and offers a boat trip to tiny Visovac Island with its Franciscan Monastery. There are many walking trails and the Krka Monastery is the spiritual centre of the Orthodox faith and sits in a bay on the Krka River.

There are several entry points into the park and in the car parks there are stalls selling souvenirs and food. There are often free samples of homemade wines, liqueurs, dried figs and almonds.

There is a good outdoor restaurant in the park which has Croatian sausages along with salads and plenty of Ozujskp, a local Croatian beer.

SPLIT TRAVEL GUIDE

Recommendations for the Budget Traveller

Places to Stay

Raspudic

Ulica Lava Nikolajeviča Tolstoja 33, 21000, Split
Tel: +385 95 906 2058

Raspudic private accommodation in Split offers a choice of rooms in three different houses across the city. All the houses are about ten minutes from the port and are just a few minutes walk from the blue flag beach.

The rooms are basic but clean and comfortable and have air conditioning and cable TV. There is a choice of twin or double rooms with shared bathroom facilities or an ensuite option if you prefer. Prices start at €11 per person per night.

Zara

Sinovčića ulica 1
21000, Split
Tel: +385 98 955 1966

This is a small family run guesthouse at the top of the city and has been in operation for six years. There is a small shop in the guesthouse to buy newspapers, drinks, souvenirs and cigarettes. Internet access is available.

There are 18 beds in double and triple bedrooms. Some rooms have ensuite facilities, air conditioning and private TV. For a stay in a double room with a shared bathroom the price per person per night is €16. Breakfast is included in the price.

Stambuk

Poljana Kneza Trpimira 2, 21000, Split
Tel: +385 91 194 4359

Stambuk is located in the heart of Split, close to the railway and bus stations as well as the ferry port and the city beaches. Close by is the Diocletian Palace and many shops, cafes and bars. The local bakery is open 24 hours a day.

There are three twin rooms available, all ensuite, and one has a private balcony. The rooms have air-conditioning, Wifi, TV, a mini cooker and mini fridge.

There is also a two bedroom apartment that sleeps up to four people. The apartment has a balcony, private bathroom and a separate toilet and a kitchen.

A stay at the Stambuk costs from €17 per person per night in a double room.

Loza

Palmina ulica 21, 21000, Split
Tel: +44 7768 110922

Staying at the Loza is more like staying at a friends house as there is just one double room in this pretty guesthouse.

The city centre is just a five minute walk away as is the port, railway and bus station. Many shops, restaurants and bars are located close by. The best city beach is a quarter of an hour away and at night the beachside area is the hub of Split's nightlife.

The ensuite double bedroom is bright and airy and has air conditioning, cable TV, fridge, Wifi and a terrace. Prices start at €17 per person per night.

Milla

Pojisanska 6
21000, Split

Milla Rooms is superbly located just 300 metres from the sandy beach and only 700m from the Diocletian Palace. Right in the heart of the city, transport links and all amenities are all within a short walk.

The rooms all recently been renovated and are bright and clean with air conditioning and a plasma TV. The larger rooms have table and chairs and all the rooms have a balcony. There is a choice of twin, double and four bedded rooms all with private bathrooms. Prices start at €12 per person per night in a four bedded room.

If you need an airport transfer the staff at Milla Rooms are happy to oblige and there is a luggage storage facility if you have a late departure.

Places to Eat & Drink

Zlatna Vrata

7 Dioklecijanova;
Tel: +385 213 45015

This is a lovaly restaurant where the aroma of pizza hits you as soon as you walk in. The wood-fired oven gives the pizzas a delightful flavour and with salads and other dishes starting at just a few kuna's you can't really go wrong.

The pretty courtyard surrounded by stone arches is a delightful place to sit and enjoy your meal and if you don't fancy pizza there is a good choice of grills, pasta and lasagna on the menu.

In the courtyard the stone steps lead to the local art house cinema Kinoteka Zlata Vrata where the chairs are adorned with celebrity names.

Zlatna Vrata is open from 8am until 11pm Monday to Saturday.

Kod Joze

4 Sredmanuska, Split
Tel: +385 213 47397

For something a little more rustic take a trip to Kod Joze. This is a family run bistro that serves hearty portions of basic, no-nonsense dishes. The family has been serving food here for thirty years at reasonable prices.

The rough stone walls and checkered tablecloths add to the cosy feeling and this is reflected in the food, it's just like you would cook at home.

Choose from seven soups or the Dalmatian ham starter before choosing your own fish from today's catch. Main courses also include grilled meats and game dishes. You can dine on a terrace as you watch the world go by or inside.

Kod Joze is open from 10am until midnight Monday to Friday and from noon until 1am Saturday and Sunday. Major credit and charge cards are accepted.

Nostromo

Kraj Svete, Marije 10, Split
Tel: +385 91 405 666
www.restoran-nostromo.hr/

This is a great place for seafood as it is operated by the owners of the fish market. Each night after trading ends the fish market becomes an upscale restaurant and the prices are very reasonable. The service is friendly and the ambience is unusual.

Try the fluffy gnocchi stuffed with fresh scampi in a garlic-flavoured soup as a starter. Choose from the array of fresh fish and seafood for your main course and round off your meal with a dessert such as the hazelnut and caramel semifreddo.

The waiters can recommend a suitable wine to match your fish.

Buffet Fife

Trumbićeva Obala 11, 21000, Split
Tel: +385 21 345 223

The focus at Fife is on grilled meat as well as fish. They serve huge portions at good prices.

It is a gathering place for backpackers, students, families and is open all day into the early hours.

The delicious homemade lemonade is recommended. Try a local speciality called *pašticada,* a beef stew that is a traditional Dalmatian dish. The tender beef is marinated overnight then cooked with cloves, nutmeg, olives and prosciutto.

Located in two small stone houses at opposite sides of the street Fife is often busy with tourists and locals. One side of the street has the kitchen and bar while the other side of the street has the indoor dining room.

For dessert try the best seller, *palacinke*, a type of sweet stuffed pancake. Even with the long opening hours of 6am until midnight it can be difficult to get a table, but it is worth the effort.

Makro Vega

Leština ulica 2,
21000, Split
Tel: +385 21 394 440
www.makrovega.hr/

Makro Vega has a Zen-like atmosphere and a good selection of beautifully presented vegan and vegetarian dishes.

There is a cosy backyard to sit outside and relax in while you enjoy a homemade lentil soup or vegetables in salsa or some of the various dishes based on tofu, mushrooms and seitan.

The brightly decorated restaurant has a daily menu and also includes a variety of vegetarian and vegan desserts and fine teas.

Makro Vega is open Monday to Friday from 9am until 9pm and on Saturday from 8am until 4pm.

Places to Shop

Fish Market (Peškarija)

The Dalmatians often prefer their food prepared in a simple fashion without exotic spices. But they like food that is fresh and locally produced. The Fish Market is the perfect place to buy this type of food.

The fish market is only open in the mornings if you fancy something fresh for dinner. The market is just to the east of Marmontova and right outside the walls of the Diocletian Palace.

The thermal baths are located very close to the fish market and legend has it that the sulfur vapours prevent the market from being overrun by flies.

The fish market is open from Monday to Saturday 7am until 1pm and on Sunday from 7am to 11am.

Green Market (Stari Pazar)

Stari Pazar is located at the opposite end of the Riva promenade to the fish market. It is close to the bus station and ferry port so makes a great place to stock up on fresh produce if you are heading over to the islands.

Leafy vegetables such as spinach and chard add deep green colour to the stalls loaded with brightly coloured and sweet-smelling tomatoes. Pomegranates, wild figs and succulent red strawberries all have a place in this medley of colours and fragrances. The produce varies with the seasons as the locals pick whatever is in their gardens and come to the market to sell it.

Cooking utensils, local brandies, olive oils, sheep's cheeses, delicious homemade preserves and jams as well as fresh poultry and cured hams and other meats can be found here as well.

There are clothes and souvenirs and the stallholders take great pride in displaying their wares in an attractive way. The market is open from 7am until 1pm.

Marmontova Shopping Street

This is the main commercial shopping street in the city and is where the famous names in fashion, footwear and fast food can be found. Many of the big designers have shops here but also look for Scandal which is an outlet offering opportunities to local designers.

Marmontova runs from the Riva waterfront to Trg Gaje Bulata and the Croatian National Theatre. With its modern plate glass shop windows and brightly lit signs there is very little to indicate Split's long history.

Among the glittering displays and fancy goods there is the oldest pharmacy in Split. Varol's dates from 1856 and is kitted out with items from an even older pharmacy in Italy. It is a good place to stop at if you are studying medicine or a similar course. There are cabinets from Renaissance times alongside figurines and old equipment which will make the visitor appreciate modern medical practice.

Along the shiny marble paved pedestrian street there are a couple of small art and photography galleries where ever-changing exhibitions show off the talent of local artists.

In an Art Nouveau building along Marmontova is the Split public spa. The outside is decorated with the works of a local architect with his rather splendid figures of naked women cavorting across the façade.

Joker

Put Brodarice 6, Split,
Tel: +385 21 396 911
www.joker.hr/

Take a 20 minute stroll from the centre of Split to Joker, a small shopping centre with around 50 shops and a cinema. The brightly lit and galleried rows of shops offer everything from trendy fashion to baby clothes, a pharmacy, an optician and toys.

On the top floor there is a restaurant, fitness club and a sky bar complete with outdoor swimming pool. Open every day from 9am to 9pm with a cinema and many bars and restaurants. There is a Kerum supermarket for grocery shopping and parking is free.

City Center One

Vukovarska ulica 207, 21000, Split
Tel: +385 21 510 130
www.citycenterone.hr

Twice the size of Joker with 110 stores spread over three floors this is the newest of Split's shopping centres and is the largest in Dalmatia.

There is parking for 2,700 cars as well as a Kid's Jungle play area, kart track and more than enough cafés and restaurants to satisfy the hungriest of diners.

In addition to designer fashion outlets there is a large Interspar hypermarket and five stores specialising in home decoration.

The centre is easy to find by car by following Vukovaska street or just take a bus. The opening hours are Monday to Sunday from 9am until 10pm.

SPLIT TRAVEL GUIDE

Printed in Great Britain
by Amazon